Words of Love

A Caregiver's Reflections through their Dementia Journey

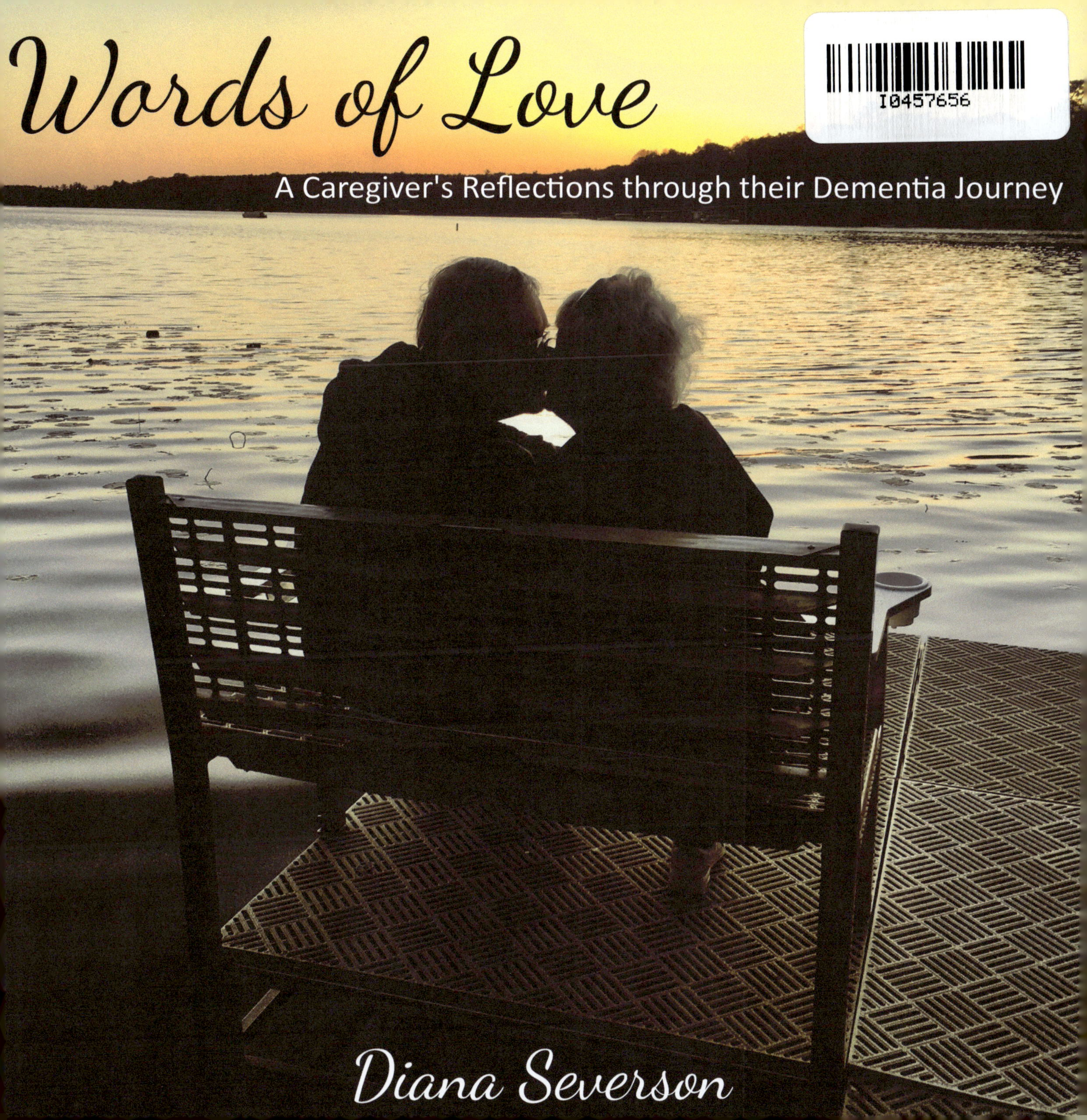

Diana Severson

First Edition
Paperback ISBN: 978-1-955541-24-4
Hardcover ISBN: 978-1-955541-25-1

Cover and interior design by Ann Aubitz
Photography by Diana Severson unless otherwise noted.
Photo, Kissing on the Dock by Bruce Boettcher. Photo, Swans on a Lake by Debbie Solomon.
Paintings by Carole Jensen.
Published by FuzionPress | 1250 E 115th Street, Burnsville, MN 55337 | fuzionpress.com | 612-781-2815

Thank you to my dear husband, family, and friends, who have walked with me through these difficult times and times of joy. I thank God for all of them each day and for carrying me through with love.

A special thanks to my dear niece, Sandy Becker, for her generous contribution to making my dream of publishing this book a reality.

I first felt inspired to write poetry in my moments of deep emotion—loss of a loved one, moments of helplessness, and so forth. With the onset of the pandemic in 2020, I began a daily habit of personal worship in the mornings. I call it my quiet time with the Lord. It has become my lifeline to get through the events of my life and this world. I could not do it without God's help.

Through sickness, tragedy, and loss, words began to come to me in my time with the Lord. Sometimes I would awaken thinking about someone I was praying for, and the words would start forming in my head. I began to get up and start writing. I have shared several of these poems with others in their time of need.

With the onset of Alzheimer's in my husband, a new area of need has arisen in me on our journey through this challenging disease. I felt the need to share some of my thoughts and feelings with others, hoping that it may enlighten and lift the burden and perhaps lead some to lean more on our heavenly Father.

There was a time, years ago, when I believed that all I had to do was believe in God and be a good person. That would ensure a good, safe, trouble-free life. I couldn't have been more wrong. I first believed in Jesus Christ as my Lord and Savior in 1974. We lived in New Jersey at the time. My husband was a traveling salesman for Brown Shoe Company. Those were good years for a while. We had two lovely young children and a pet dog living in a nice suburban neighborhood.

Though far away from our extended family in Minnesota, we were prepared to raise our children there. That changed suddenly when my husband lost his job at Brown Shoe Company, and we were forced to decide where we wanted our future to progress from there. We decided to put the house up for sale and return to Minnesota and our roots. My husband was promised a job there and went on ahead to begin the process.

While alone in New Jersey, I suddenly realized what I was missing! I was reading a book by Catherine Marshall, and some words jumped out at me. I hadn't given my heart and soul to Jesus Christ as my Lord and Savior. I prayed on the spot, beginning a great adventure and new direction in my life. I soon learned that my previous belief about not having problems in this world was a misconception. We had many years ahead of some of the most difficult challenges I have ever faced. I learned quickly that when Jesus said, "In this world, you will have troubles," he was right. I also eventually learned that his promise, "But take heart, I have overcome the world," was deep and true.

Now I know that the Holy Spirit lives and dwells in me and has inspired me to write poetry in the hope that someone, somewhere, will be touched by it and learn to lean on the Lord and be comforted in His care. It is my prayer that this book will bless all who read it.

Peace and love,

Diana Severson

Be still and know that I am God.
Psalm 46:10

Be Still and Know I am God

Oh Lord, my heart cries out to you,
    in this world full of strife.
Come close to those who need you now
    amidst their stressful times of life.
So hard to see your love flow free,
    among the ruins of tragedy,
surrounding this cruel world today,
    Oh, give us strength to hope and pray.
You will sustain in your great way.
    I love you, Lord, and this I know.
You love us more than we can grasp.
    So when you come in glory soon,
our hearts so filled with joy will be,
    to spend with you eternity.
Just peace and love and beauty see,
    so, Maranatha, Lord, I say.
Come, Lord Jesus, we await,
    for on that day, all sin abates.
No more pain or sorrow, see,
    only light, and love, and joy, in Thee.

A Prayer in Illness

Oh, precious Lord, please hear my prayer,
    and bless our loved one, dear.
Please hold him very close to you,
    and wash away his fear.
Let him feel your presence, Lord,
    and give him strength he needs,
to face the path ahead for him,
    so very hard indeed.
And bless our family, dear Lord,
    and keep them in your care.
So very, very difficult,
    the burden they must bear.
To watch one suffer in this life,
    even with your Grace.
So, give them strength when they are weak.
    Guide them daily, you to seek.
Heal their pain and love them true,
    as you have said you'd always do.
Never leave them or forsake them.
    You have promised in your Word.
So come now, Lord, your love afford
    them peace through all that they must face.
God bless them, Lord.
    Surround them always with your Grace.

Let the morning bring me word of your unfailing love.
Psalm 143

The Lord is close to the brokenhearted and saves those who are crushed in spirit.
Psalm 34:18

The Long Goodbye

Dementia's cruel, dementia's sad.
　　It steals one's mind away.
It takes away the memories dear, that we once shared each day.
　　Oh Lord my God, I cannot help but wonder, ponder, pray.
I ask you why this evil plight continues on each day.
　　It cuts so deep and lonely, Lord, to each one in its way.
Oh, please, my Lord, my Savior, dear.
　　I know you walk with me
amidst the pain and sorrow felt.
　　You're always ever near.
Restore my strength and give me faith,
　　that you will see me through.
Just as your word doth saith,
　　I know that you will do,
what's best for me and loved one, dear.
　　Holy Spirit, walk me through,
and be Thou always ever near.

You will seek me and find me
when you seek me with
all your heart.
JEREMIAH 29:13

Jesus With Me

Jesus, hear me when I call.
　　Hear me whisper when I pray.
You are love, my Lord, my all,
　　with me each and every day.
My heart cries out, oh, Holy One.
　　I know your will on earth be done.
I pray you help my loved one dear,
　　to overcome his angst and fear.
I know you love him through and through.
　　The plan behind in all you do,
is love and mercy, kindness true.
　　From all his fear, you will release,
all bonds that hold him in their grip.
　　Fill him head to toe with peace and love
that comes from only God above.
　　So filled with hope, let me now be,
trusting now, my Lord in Thee.

Love Me to You, Jesus

Lord, oh Lord, my heart cries out to you,
    who loves beyond a doubt.
Blot out this loneliness in me.
    I know that it comes not from Thee.
Instead, restore to me thy rope of hope,
    that anchors me to you in love,
and to my heavenly home above.
    Give me strength when I am weak.
Help me always, You, to seek,
    to fill the gaps of love in me,
and fill me to the brim with Thee.
    No more loneliness nor dread.
My heart at peace with you instead.
    Come, Lord Jesus, three in one.
Hold me close and love, love, love.
    Til my work on earth is done.

Our anchor is not located in the deepest sea but in the highest heaven.
HEBREWS 6:19

Help me, Lord, this I Pray

The days grow long, the nights as well,
    and what comes next is hard to tell.
It's like a roller coaster, that's for sure,
    and it gets harder to endure.
If not for love so deep and long,
    I don't know how I'd carry on.
The man I know is gone away,
    and now a new one here to stay.
The questions rise within my heart,
    how did this illness so impart.
A task I surely could not do,
    without my Lord, my friends, so true.
So help me, Lord, and guide my way.
    Be with me now and every day.
Give me your love for him so free,
    and get my focus off of me.
I love you, Lord, so help me now,
    to do the things that I did vow,
in marriage very long ago,
    and will continue more so now.

Show me your ways, oh Lord,
teach me your paths, guide me in your truth,
and teach me, for You are God, my Savior, and
my hope is in You all the day long.
Psalm 25:4,5

Times Gone By

My precious love, I miss you so.
    My heart is wrenched in two,
for you no longer share with me,
    the things we used to do.
I miss you more and more each day.
    Fill my heart, oh Lord, I pray,
with love unselfish, stayed and true,
    and let me not forget the real, true you.
This cruel disease, it steals away,
    the memories once dear.
It leaves behind a brand new you
    to be with ever near.
Sometimes good, and sometimes not,
    I know that you are there.
The man I always loved before
    is still in there somewhere.
Oh, give me strength to carry on
    along this weary ride.
To love you still, no matter what,
    and be there by your side.
I thank you, Lord, my one, my all.
    Without you near, I could not do,
this task for which you call.
    Give me the patience, love, I plea.
Remind me that you walk with me.
    So hold my hand, for you I seek,
and carry me when I am weak.
    For you have said in your sweet word,
When I am weak, then you are strong.
    So hear me, precious Lord, I pray,
and always carry me along.

The Lord is my rock, my fortress,
and my deliverer, my God in
whom I take refuge.
PSALM 18:2

Dreams of Long Ago

At times I feel so isolated.
I know this cannot be abated.
Though I have been so truly blessed
with loved ones, friends, and all the rest,
It still feels sad and lonely, Lord,
for this is not my chosen task to do.
So, help me, Lord, to cling to you.
Guide me through the tempest true.
so far, from all my dreams we'd do,
and all the things we would pursue.
I know you have a plan for me.
Help me now to trust in Thee.
Give me strength when I am weak.
Help me always you to seek.
I need you, Lord, oh this I know.
Be with me now, where ere I go.

For I know the plans I have for
you declares the Lord, plans to prosper you,
and not to harm you, plans to give
you hope and a future.
Jer 29:11

To Carry on Day by Day

Oh Lord, my Lord, I cannot say,
    how much I need Thee every day.
The nights are hard with little sleep.
    So sad to watch, it cuts so deep.
I love him so, my husband dear,
    though he is still so very near,
he's far away from who I knew.
    in everything he now doth do.
He's sweet at times when at his best.
    I cannot tell what will come next.
A roller coaster, that's for sure.
    Please help me, Lord, to just endure.
His needs are many, I am one.
    It seems much harder to get done,
all the care that he does need.
    requires the best of me indeed.
And so, dear Lord,
    Please be my strength.
Help me please to carry on,
    for now and to whatever length,
this journey doth prolong.

For nothing will be impossible with God.
Luke 1:37

Tears of Love

Oh, Lord, how sad it is to see.
   the one I love who used to be,
my friend, my go-to person, sure,
   now struggling so, to just endure.
He still shows love and kindness, yes,
   when he is feeling at his best,
but seems so lost in many ways,
   so often, on so many days.
My heart does break to see him so
   befuddled as he strives to know,
the things that used to come to him,
   so naturally, and now so dim.
God bless him, Lord, and give him peace.
   Surround him in your love with ease.
Let him feel your loving arms,
   around him tight to never cease.

Those who sow in tears
will reap with songs of joy.
Psalm 126:5

God is our refuge and
strength, a very present help
in trouble.
PSALM 46:1

My Heart Cries Out

Oh Lord, My Lord, my heart cries out.
    It goes from joy, and peace, so fast,
My mind doth speed and spin about
    to things of earth that do not last.
I am so tired dear, dear one.
    I once again implore your strength.
Please lift me up and carry me
    for yet another time and length.
My "golden years," they once were called,
    not so golden after all.
Without you, Lord, I'd surely fall.
    Please hold me close and lead me on
the path you've chosen just for me.
    Hold my hand here and beyond.
Let me trust what I can't see.
    Knowing what you've promised true,
that is surely what you'll do.
    Bless my loved ones with your care.
Fill their hearts with love for you.
    Let me lay them at your throne,
for you to guide in all they do.

My Heart is Torn in Two

Oh, Lord, my heart is torn in two.
    I really don't know what to do.
This awful illness he must bear
    tugs at my heartstrings everywhere.
At times he is so frightened sad, and weak,
    and words he finds so hard to speak.
Those he loves, he's not so clear
    of who they are, and who is near.
It's up and down the feeling scales.
    Sometimes I wish that I could wail.
But in this life, I do so know,
    sometimes it's hard to see it though,
that you are truly love supreme,
    and have a plan for him to glean.
Please love him, Lord, and give him peace.
    Give me strength to never cease,
to care for him so lovingly,
    that he will feel your love through me.

So clothe yourselves with
compassion, kindness, humility,
gentleness, and patience.
Colossians 3:12

Help Me, Jesus, on this Day

Help me, Jesus, on this day.
　　Guide my steps along the way.
For I am weak, and you are strong.
　　In your loving arms do I belong,
for you're the one, and you're the all,
　　that bled to keep me from the fall.
So help me trust you, Savior sweet,
　　in all I say and all I do.
May I always bring you glory, honor you.
　　Oh, praise be yours, oh precious one,
For all that you have said and done.
　　Glory be to you on high.
Help me trust that you are nigh.

Trust in the Lord with all your
heart and lean not on your own
understanding.
PROVERBS 3:5

You will seek me and find me
when you seek me with all
your heart.
JEREMIAH 29:13

I need you, Lord

Oh Lord, please hear me when I pray,
　　for I don't know just what to do.
This added burden now he bears,
　　of pain to catch him through and through.
It feels too much to add to this
　　already cru-el fate.
As if dementia's not enough
　　for him that he must take.
I do my best to comfort him,
　　to help relieve the pain,
but soon it's back ferociously,
　　just when I thought we'd made a gain.
I need you, Lord, to help him, please.
　　His pain to truly ease.
Please touch him with your holy hand,
　　and make the pain to cease.
For nothing is impossible
　　for you, my Savior dear.
So help me to remember this
　　and know you're always near.
You love him even more than I,
　　this I know for sure.
You've promised often in your Word
　　that we, you'll help endure,
whatever comes to us each day,
　　in your own special way.
And so I thank you once again.
　　Let me ne'er forget,
your promise true, and say Amen,
　　once again to You.

Love is patient,
love is kind.
2 CORINTHIANS:4

Feelings

Help me, Lord, for this, I pray.
    Make resentment go away.
I know the one who tries me so,
    is still the one that I love so.
It is so difficult to stay
    calm and understanding every day.
The challenges they do build so,
    I often feel as though I'd blow.
At times it's oh so difficult
    to smile and to agree,
Though many things he says to me,
    I truly cannot see.
The constant, constant cries of pain,
    that so far now are unexplained.
It's very hard to know what's real
    and which ones he must really feel.
He can't express his feelings true,
    so I don't know just what to do.
So give me patience to endure,
    and yet be kind and nice for sure.
I need you more and more each day
    to chart this path ahead for me.
Be with me, Lord, again I pray,
    and guide my steps to walk with Thee.

He is Always There

When life throws curves that knock you down,
    remember He, whose arms surround.
Always loving, kind, and true,
    He will always get you through.
Though the path at times seems hard,
    in the end, you'll know for sure,
He was with you to endure.
    He is there to guide and guard.
So come now, child, and trust and know,
    that I am always where you go.
I will guide your every step.
    Put one foot first and then the next.
For all is mine, and mine is all.
    Nothing is too hard for me.
I will always lead you to,
    exactly where you need to be.
I love you, child, now, rest in peace,
    and know my love will never cease.
Though hard times in this world will be,
    one day soon, you will be here,
to walk and talk and live with me.
    Remember, this world full of strife,
overcome, already done,
    by my great act of love and grace,
will guarantee for you a place.
    Hang on to hope and let it be, fully
strong with trust in me.
    Because you know that you will see,
life with me eternally.

Therefore, we do
not lose heart.
2 COR: 16

For we know that these light and
momentary troubles are achieving
for us an eternal glory that
outweighs them all.
2 COR: 17

Give thanks to the Lord, for he is
good. His love endures forever.
PSALM 118:1

Gratitude

My heart is full of gratitude to You,
    my Lord, my one, my all,
for all the things you say and do,
    to keep me from the fall,
into the depths of sorrow deep,
    from where return is slow.
I trust in You, my Savior dear,
    for there is nothing You don't know.
You have my back, of this, I'm sure,
    in all things great and small.
Always at my side, you'll be,
    helping me endure.
Whatever comes my way, dear Lord,
    you will know it all,
and make a way for me to cope.
    With You, by my side, I know,
You'll always be my one true hope.
    So, thank you, Lord, for loving me,
so very, very much.
    For being in my life each day,
my heart, You do so touch.

Blessings

Thank you, God, for loved ones, friends,
     who help to guide me through,
all the twists and turns and bends,
     without them, I could not do.
The loneliness this illness brings,
     so hard it is to bear.
But knowing you are at my side,
     and always will be there,
helps me to carry on, dear Lord,
     knowing that you care.
Although, at times, I still do ponder,
     why you allow this cru-el fate.
Yet I know your plans of wonder,
     goes beyond my lowly state.
I trust you, Lord, to carry me,
     and give me strength that I so need,
until at last, I finally see,
     you face to face eternally.
No more crying, no more pain,
     tears and death there will not be.
For in your Word, you do so claim,
     that God will reign forever more,
In perfect love and harmony.

He will wipe every tear from their
eyes. There will be no more death
or mourning, or crying, or pain.
REVELATION 21:4

Forgive me, Lord

Oh, Lord my Lord, I'm so ashamed.
    I know that it's not fair for him to blame,
for acting out behavior, mean,
    toward me, and me alone, it seems.
His moods they change like night and day.
    Sometimes I don't know what to say.
At times his anger pierces deep.
    My coping skills are hard to keep.
I know it is not him, I see.
    That deep inside the true man be.
The man I love with all my heart,
    today and always from the start.
However, hard it is to keep
    from lashing out when hurt is deep.
I must remember, help me please,
    to love him, see him with your eyes.
Please help me do it more with ease.
    Holy Spirit, need you so.
Guide me on my way to go.
    Often times it makes me sad.
At other times, it makes me mad.
    But I know, Lord, that you are there,
in me, for me, everywhere.
    Forgive me Lord when I react.
Help me keep my moods intact.

You, Lord are forgiving and good,
abounding in love to all
who call to you.
PSALM 86:5

Treasures in My Trials

Day by day, my loved one fails,
    it is so hard to see.
Sometimes I don't know if I can,
    continue this path laid for me.
Oh Lord my God, please let me feel
    your presence here with me.
I wish that I could feel your hand,
    that tethers me to Thee.
I often wonder why, I'm on this path in life,
    but then I am reminded that
you said this world has strife.
    Let me remember what you said,
"This world you've overcome."
    And carry on with love each day
until my work is done.
    There's treasures in my trials, you've said,
so help me always know,
    your joy, amidst the struggle here,
and guide me as I go.
    I fix my eyes on Jesus pure,
and worry fades away.
    He's holding me in love so dear.
He's sure to lead the way.

In this world, you will have trouble,
but take heart, I have
overcome the world.
John 16:33

Come, Lord Jesus,

Come, Lord Jesus, be with me.
    Let me feel your comfort free.
Peace within I so long for,
    let your Spirit deep within me soar.
This life here on earth is hard.
    I could not do without your guard.
I know your grace sufficient' s true,
    for me, in all, I say and do.
Yet, still, at times, I wander far
    and seem to wonder where you are.
Forgive me, Lord; you know I care
    and know that you are everywhere.
My flesh gets in the way, I know,
    confusing so, the way to go.
I need you so much every day.
    Holy Spirit, reign in me profound,
and o'er my flesh, You will abound.
    Bless this day and fill it full
of love and deep, deep trust in you.
    Help me always to remember
you are there to see me through.

My Grace is sufficient for you, for
my power is made perfect
in weakness.
2 CORINTHIANS 12:9

Show me the way I should go,
for to you, I lift up my soul.
Psalm 143:8b

Oh God, I Need You Now

Oh God, my God, I need you now.
   Help me, guide me, show me how
to patiently keep on,
   in trusting You beyond,
what day-to-day does bring,
   trusting You in everything.
Oh Lord, I'm here on bended knee,
   asking, I know, much of Thee.
But sometimes, Lord, I just don't know,
   how much further I can go.
Give me strength and keep me wise.
   Help me see him with your eyes,
and with your heart to love him true,
   just as I know well you do.
This disease, it really stings
   and hurts so badly every way.
Heal the pain it often brings.
   Replace the pain with love this day.
Your promises, please let me keep,
   well within my heart, so very deep.
You have said to love, love, love,
   here on earth and soon above.
Though hard to do with human flesh,
   dear Holy Spirit, do the rest.
Be with me now throughout this day,
   leading me along the way.

The Lord bless you and keep you,
the Lord make his face to shine
upon you and be gracious to you.
NUMBERS 6: 24,25

God Bless and Keep Him

God bless and keep him on this day.
    Be sure and show us both the way,
to take each step and always know,
    that You are there where ere we go.
Remove the fear and angst he feels.
    Fill the gaps of peace for him
with your love and peace within.
    Let him know your grace doth seal,
your promise of eternity surreal.
    Wrap your arms around him, Lord,
love him to you tenderly.
    Step by step, please hold his hand,
and let him know you'll always be,
    there for him through thick and thin.
Let him feel you deep within,
    his heart and soul, true peace to win.
Thank you, Lord; now let us be,
    consecrated Lord to Thee.

Lord, Change my Heart

Lord, take captive every thought I hear
    that's not from you and doth cause fear.
Replace it with your thoughts of love
    and promises from up above.
Fill me Holy Spirit through,
    to toes and fingertips complete.
Show me, please, what I must do
    to stay within your will so sweet.
I know your love does not sow fear,
    but fills me up with hope instead,
and takes me where You want me led,
    To You, dear Lord, I lift my soul.
Trust in You doth be my goal.
    Every day and every hour,
let me ne'er forget your power.
    Nothing is impossible for you.
You will always see me through.

I can do everything through Him
who gives me strength.
Phil 4: 13

Moments

The moments on the porch,
    while in your arms I lay,
snuggled up and cozy,
    to start anew the day.
Listening to the bubbling pond,
    peace and quiet all around,
good feelings, they abound.
    Help me always to hold on,
to moments such as these,
    that happen so with ease,
reflecting on them far beyond,
    when I no longer see,
the same affection I so love,
    come from you to me.
Fill the gaps with your great love,
    Lord Jesus, hear my plea,
and shower love from up above.

And now these three remain faith, hope,
and love. But the greatest of these is love.
1 Corinthians 13:13

It is my prayer that this book
will bless all who read it.
Peace and love,

Diana Severson

www.ingramcontent.com/pod-product-compliance
Lightning Source LLC
Chambersburg PA
CBHW041556120626
46551CB00002B/229